What is in this book?

Energy!

We are living things. Plants and animals are living things. Living things need air, sunlight, and water to stay alive. Living things also need energy. Energy is the power we need to move.

What is a Food Chain?

Bobbie Kalman

Dalmatian Press

Created by Bobbie Kalman

Published in 2013 by Dalmatian Press, LLC, Franklin, TN 37068-2068.
1-866-418-2572. DalmatianPress.com
Printed in China

CE16260/1012

Author and Editor-in-Chief
Bobbie Kalman

Reading Consultant
Elaine Hurst
Joan King
Jennifer King

Editors
Kathy Middleton
Crystal Sikkens

Photo research
Bobbie Kalman

Illustrations
Barbara Bedell: page 23

Photographs
Corel: page 15 (bottom)
Photos.com: page 5
other photographs by Shutterstock.

Plants need energy to grow and make new plants. Animals need energy to move, grow, find food, and stay safe.

Food energy

Food gives plants, animals, and people the energy they need. The energy in food comes from the sun.

This girl is standing in a wheat field. She is holding bread made from wheat. Wheat gets energy from the sun.

It starts with plants

People and animals cannot use the energy from sunlight to make food. Only plants can make food with the sun's energy. Plants have a special green color in their leaves, called **chlorophyll**. Chlorophyll catches sunlight.

Chlorophyll absorbs the sun's energy.

What is that word?

Plants use sunlight, air, water, and nutrients from the soil to grow and make food. A very long word describes how plants make food from sunlight. The word is **photosynthesis**.

Chlorophyll gives this leaf its green color.

A plant's leaves
catch sunlight.
A plant's leaves
take in air.
The leaves let
out fresh air.
soil
water

Energy flows

Animals and people have to get the sun's energy from plants. When an animal eats a plant, the sun's stored energy flows from the plant to the animal.

When these bees eat the nectar in flowers, they are getting a product of the sun's energy. Nectar is a sweet liquid inside flowers.

What is an herbivore?

An **herbivore** is an animal that eats plants. Herbivores eat different kinds of plants and different parts of plants. This squirrel is eating the seeds of a flower. It is getting the sun's energy from the seeds.

The rabbit is eating grass.
The porcupine will eat these flowers.

What is a carnivore?

Some animals do not eat plants. They eat other animals. Animals that eat other animals are called **carnivores**.

The grasshopper is eating a plant. The chameleon will eat the grasshopper.

The spider is going to eat the fly.
The snake is eating a frog.

What is a food chain?

A **food chain** is the passing of the sun's energy from one living thing to another.

The food chain starts with plants.

Next, the energy goes into the rabbit that eats the plants.

When the lynx eats the rabbit, the sun's energy is passed along to the lynx.

The plants, rabbit, and lynx make up the food chain.

sun
energy
plant
energy
rabbit
energy
lynx

A food web

Animals eat more than one kind of food, just as you do. When they eat different foods, they belong to more than one food chain.

When two or more food chains are in one place, there is a **food web**. The food web on the next page is in a forest.

Foxes eat squirrels and chipmunks.

Cougars eat squirrels and chipmunks.

Squirrels and chipmunks eat nuts and seeds.

Nuts and seeds contain the sun's energy.

What do they eat?

Some of these animals eat both plants and animals. They are called **omnivores**. Guess which of these animals are omnivores.

ANSWER

They are all omnivores!

Index